PLAY LIKE THE PROS

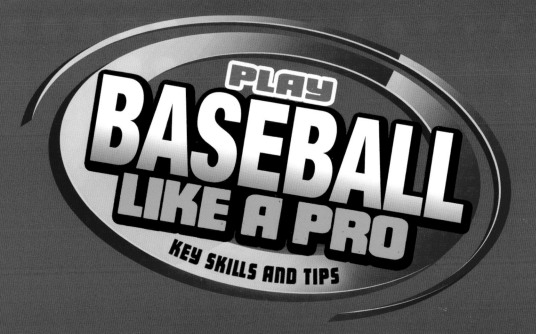

PLAY BASEBALL LIKE A PRO
KEY SKILLS AND TIPS

BY HANS HETRICK

Consultant:
Jeffrey L. Chambers
Head Athletic Trainer
Minnesota State University
Mankato, Minnesota

CAPSTONE PRESS
a capstone imprint

Sports Illustrated KIDS Play Like the Pros is published by Capstone Press,
1710 Roe Crest Drive, North Mankato, Minnesota 56003
www.capstonepub.com

Books published by Capstone Press are manufactured with paper
containing at least 10 percent post-consumer waste.

Library of Congress Cataloging-in-Publication Data
Hetrick, Hans, 1973–
    Play baseball like a pro: key skills and tips / By Hans Hetrick.
    p. cm.—(Sports illustrated kids : play like the pros)
    Includes bibliographical references and index.
    Summary: "Provides instructional tips on how to improve one's
baseball skills, including quotes and advice from professional coaches
and athletes"—Provided by publisher.
    ISBN 978-1-4296-4824-0 (library binding)
    ISBN 978-1-4296-5644-3 (paperback)
1. Baseball—Training—Juvenile literature. I. Title. II. Series.
GV867.5.H48 2011
796.357071—dc22   2010007241

EDITORIAL CREDITS

Aaron Sautter and Anthony Wacholtz, editors; Ted Williams, designer;
    Eric Gohl, media researcher; Laura Manthe, production specialist

PHOTO CREDITS

Capstone Studio/Karon Dubke, 8 (bottom), 10 (bottom)
Shutterstock/kentoh, design element; Morgan Lane Photography, cover, 3 (baseball);
    Vjom, design element
Sports Illustrated/Al Tielemans, 13, 21 (bottom), 25; Bob Rosato, 12, 21 (top);
    Chuck Solomon, 4–5, 19, 28 (bottom); Damian Strohmeyer, 7, 11, 17 (top),
    24 (top), 26; David E. Klutho, 9 (top), 24 (bottom); John Biever, 6 (top), 8 (top),
    14, 18; John Iacono, cover (right), 15 (right), 16, 20; John W. McDonough,
    6 (bottom), 15 (left), 17 (bottom), 27, 28 (top); Peter Read Miller, 22;
    Robert Beck, cover (left), 9 (bottom), 23 (all); Simon Bruty, 10 (top)

Printed in the United States of America in North Mankato, Minnesota.
012012   006581

TABLE OF CONTENTS

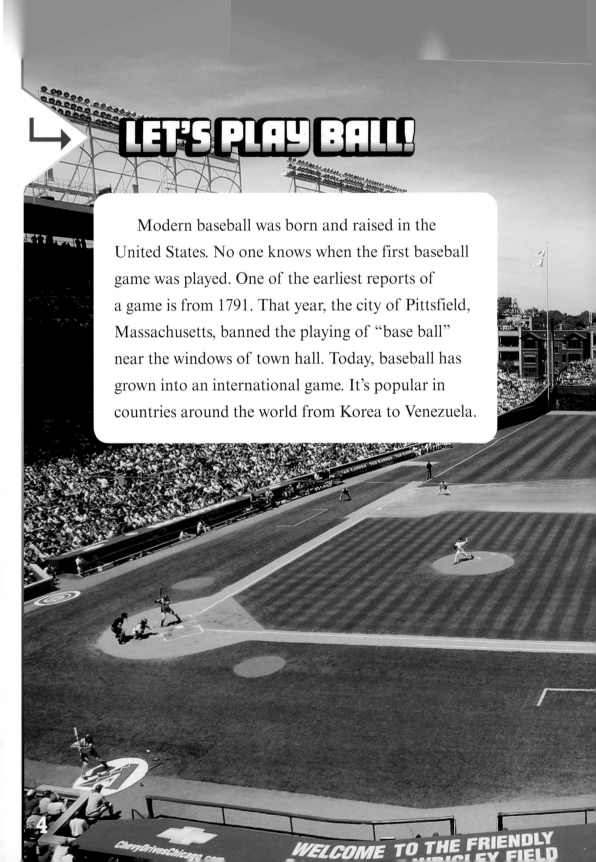

LET'S PLAY BALL!

Modern baseball was born and raised in the United States. No one knows when the first baseball game was played. One of the earliest reports of a game is from 1791. That year, the city of Pittsfield, Massachusetts, banned the playing of "base ball" near the windows of town hall. Today, baseball has grown into an international game. It's popular in countries around the world from Korea to Venezuela.

ChevyDrivesChicago.com

WELCOME TO THE FRIENDLY
WRIGLEY FIELD

Professional baseball players come in many sizes. They can be big and strong like Albert Pujols, or they can be small and quick like Dustin Pedroia. But there is one quality all great baseball players share—they are mentally tough. As Yogi Berra famously joked, "Baseball is 90 percent mental, and the other half is physical."

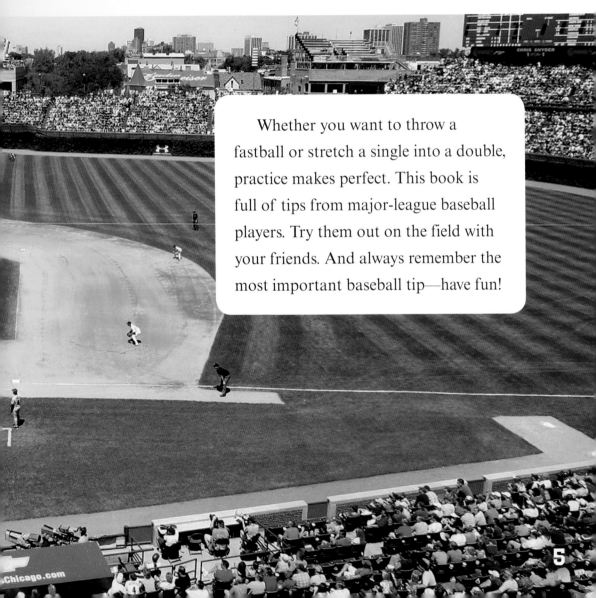

Whether you want to throw a fastball or stretch a single into a double, practice makes perfect. This book is full of tips from major-league baseball players. Try them out on the field with your friends. And always remember the most important baseball tip—have fun!

Chicago.com

START WITH THE BASICS

Evan Longoria makes it look easy when he snatches a hard line drive and snaps the ball to first base for the out. Years of practice help pro baseball players make amazing plays. But even after they get to the big leagues, they continue to practice and learn about the game of baseball.

LISTEN AND OBSERVE

Coaches are there to help players. Ask your coaches questions about improving your play. Listen to them and put their advice into action. When you're watching a game, follow the players closely and make notes. What did they do right? What did they do wrong?

BE PATIENT

Baseball is a difficult game. A fraction of an inch can mean the difference between a base hit and an out. Don't become frustrated. Perfecting skills takes time and determination.

BE PREPARED FOR THE UNEXPECTED

Crazy things often happen in baseball. Good players make bad throws. The wind can push the ball in unexpected directions. But if you pay attention, you'll be ready to take an extra base or make a tough catch.

"Patience is key. A lot of people want [success] fast. It's not going to work out when you want it, but it'll be there. You will be rewarded. You have to go through struggle to have progress."
-TORII HUNTER, OUTFIELDER, LOS ANGELES ANGELS

2 HOW TO PAINT THE CORNERS

Not every major-league pitcher can throw a fastball that travels 95 miles per hour (mph). Many star pitchers, like the Philadelpia Phillies' Jamie Moyer, have incredible control over their pitches. Practice these tips and soon you'll be "painting the corners" of the plate with pinpoint strikes.

FOUR-SEAM GRIP

For the best control of a fastball, use the four-seam grip. Hold the baseball so the horseshoe shape of the seams is sideways. Lay your first two fingers across the top of the ball with your fingertips on the seams. Place your other fingers next to the bottom curve of the horseshoe.

DON'T MOVE YOUR HEAD

If your head is out of control, your body will be too. If your body is out of control, so is your pitching arm. Stay balanced. Keep your head directly over your body. And be sure to keep your eyes on the catcher's mitt until the pitch is hit or caught.

SHADOW PITCH

Practice pitching without the ball. Go through your whole delivery. That way you can concentrate on the motion of your body instead of where the ball goes.

Superior Speed ▶

Since 2000, many major-league pitchers have broken 100 mph on the radar gun. Although many baseball experts doubt the accuracy of radar guns, few question the power of Joel Zumaya's fastball. The Detroit Tigers relief pitcher threw a 103-mph fastball in 2006. It was the fastest pitch ever recorded during a major-league game.

3 HOW TO THROW A CHANGEUP

The changeup is a difficult pitch for batters to hit. It looks exactly like a fastball, but it's much slower. Usually the batter will swing long before the ball crosses the plate. Throwing a changeup is called "pulling the string." The pitch looks like the pitcher has the ball on a string. Then he seems to pull it back just before the batter swings.

CIRCLE CHANGE

The most popular changeup is the circle change. It gets its name from the grip. Place your thumb and index finger on the side of the baseball and make a circle. Place your pinkie on the other side of the ball.

TIGHTER GRIP

The changeup is slower than a fastball because the grip is tighter. Keep your index finger and pinkie fairly tight on the ball as you release it. Let the ball

roll off your middle and ring finger.

The changeup is a "feel" pitch. You will need a lot of practice to find the right pressure to put on your grip.

FASTBALL ARM SPEED

Throw the changeup with the same arm speed as a fastball. The grip and the release will slow down the ball. If you throw it with fastball arm speed, the batter will expect a fastball.

"Hitting is timing; pitching is upsetting timing."
-WARREN SPAHN, HALL OF FAME PITCHER, BOSTON/MILWAUKEE BRAVES

4 HOW TO SACRIFICE BUNT

There's no glory in a sacrifice bunt. It doesn't improve your statistics, and you probably will be thrown out at first. But sacrifice bunts are still important. They move the runners to the next base. Good bunters earn their team's trust and respect. These tips will help you lay down a perfect bunt.

SQUARE UP

After the pitcher starts the wind up, square your shoulders, face the pitcher, and bend your knees. This stance will help you see the ball better. Your body and arms will also be closer to the ball when it comes in over the plate.

SLIDE YOUR HAND UP

Slide your top hand up the barrel of the bat for better control. You'll be able to adjust the angle of the bat to tap the ball down a baseline.

"CATCH" THE BALL

When the ball hits the bat, soften the bunt. Bring the bat back like you're catching the pitch. Don't hit the ball too hard. If you bunt the ball too far, the fielder will have a chance to throw out the runners on base.

"Your job above all is to get the bunt down. You square around and get your bat angle set a little earlier. Then concentrate on seeing the ball."
JUAN PIERRE, OUTFIELDER, CHICAGO WHITE SOX

5 HOW TO HIT A CURVEBALL

A curveball is much slower than a fastball. It's never an easy pitch to hit, whether from a right-handed or a left-handed pitcher. Work on these tips and you'll see some of those curveballs fall right into your bat.

IDENTIFY IT

It's not too difficult to spot a curveball. If you watch closely, you will see the pitcher's wrist turn and his arm come across his body. The pitch will also be slower than other pitches.

After a lot of fastballs, your body will want to swing at fastball speed. But you have to wait on a curveball. If you start your swing too quickly, you won't be able to recover. Ignore your instincts and let the ball come to you.

STAND STILL

Waiting to swing is hard to do when the curveball is coming right at you. But don't fall out of your batting stance. Stay still until the ball begins to curve. When it does, you'll know where it's going. If it's a good pitch, take your swing.

6 HOW TO SLIDE INTO HOME

A play at home plate is one of the most exciting plays in baseball. The difference between an out and a run can be decided in a split second. When you're running for home and the play is close, try sliding into the plate. It's a great way to avoid the catcher's tag.

SLIDE OUTSIDE

Slide into home plate feetfirst on the outside of the baseline. The catcher will have to reach farther to tag you. Remember, base runners are allowed to be 3 feet (0.9 meters) away from the baseline.

HOOK THE LEG

When you slide past the catcher, hook your left leg back. Touch home plate with your toe. Keep the rest of your body as far away from the catcher as you can.

HEADFIRST SLIDE

Headfirst slides can also be valuable in avoiding the tag. Slide past the catcher on the outside of the base path. Then reach out your left hand to touch home plate.

HOW TO BREAK UP A DOUBLE PLAY

As a runner on first base, it's your job to keep the defense from making a **double play**. If you slide hard into second base, the hitter has a better chance of making it to first. Follow these tips to make it hard for the other team to turn two.

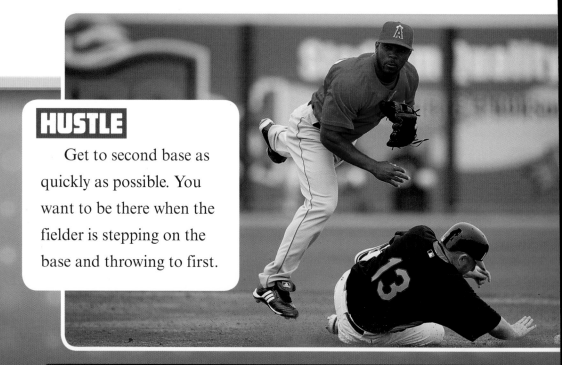

HUSTLE

Get to second base as quickly as possible. You want to be there when the fielder is stepping on the base and throwing to first.

↳ **double play**—when the team on defense gets two outs on a single play

SLIDE INTO THE FIELDER'S FEET

Slide feetfirst into the legs of the fielder covering second base. You don't want to hurt the fielder. You just want to keep him from stepping into the throw. Aim your slide where the fielder is going to step.

STAY CLOSE

You can slide over second base or next to it to disrupt the fielder's throw. But don't slide too far away from the base. The rules state that your hand must be able to touch the base at the end of your slide. If you're too far away, both you and the batter will be called out.

HOW TO DEFEND HOME PLATE

The catcher is a baseball team's last line of defense. When a runner heads for home, the catcher needs to block the plate, catch the ball, and apply the tag. Catchers need to be ready for anything. Some runners will try to slide around them. Others will lower their shoulder and try to jar the ball loose from the catcher's grasp. Use these tips to help keep the other team off the scoreboard.

BLOCK THE PLATE

Put your left foot in front of home plate and face the baseball. After you catch the ball, drop your knee in front of the base so your shin guard is blocking the plate. When you block home plate, the runner will have to go through you or around you.

CATCH THE BALL

Make sure you make the catch. You can't tag out the runner without the ball. When you have the ball, go after the runner and apply the tag.

STAY LOW

Bend your knees. If the runner hits you, this position will give you more balance and help you absorb the shock. If the runner slides, you'll be low to the ground so you can apply the tag quickly.

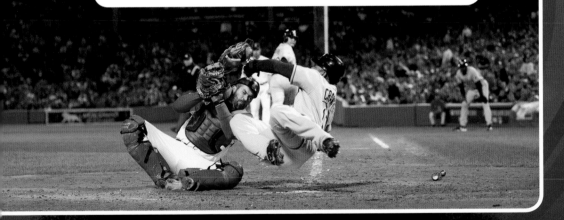

"A runner can try and run you over or slide around you. You need to be ready for either. Ideally, you want to stay down and present a low center of gravity."

HENRY BLANCO, CATCHER, NEW YORK METS

9 HOW TO THROW OUT A BASE STEALER

Catchers are sometimes called the field generals. If you're a catcher, you're in charge of controlling the action on the field. A big part of being the catcher is keeping base runners from stealing. When runners try to steal a base, catchers try to throw them out. Here are a couple of tips to keep base runners in check.

RAISE YOUR CROUCH

When a runner is on base, raise your catcher's crouch stance. Lift your backside up like you're leaning forward on a small chair. In a higher crouch, you can pop up quickly to throw the ball.

POINT YOUR TOE AT THE BASE

When the runner tries to steal, pop up with your lead toe pointing at the base. With your toe pointed in the right direction, your body will come around correctly when you throw. Your throw will be more accurate.

THROW LOW

Your throw should be low. You want the ball to hit your teammate's glove just above the ground on the right side of the base. This is where the runner will slide into the base. If you hit the right spot, your teammate should be able to get the tag and the out.

"If you have a strong arm, you have a big advantage for throwing guys out. But if you don't have a strong arm, it really helps to have quick legs."
-IVAN "PUDGE" RODRIGUEZ, CATCHER, TEXAS RANGERS

Turning a double play is an exciting part of playing shortstop. The second baseman snags a hard grounder. Then he flips it to the shortstop, who has run to second base. The shortstop then throws it to first. In a flash, two runners are thrown out in just one play. Here are a couple of tips to help you turn two from the shortstop position.

CATCH THE BALL ON THE MOVE

Stay a few steps behind second base until the ball is thrown to you. Catch the ball on the base and throw on the move. The extra speed will give your throw extra power.

SQUARE UP TO THE FIELDER

You will usually have plenty of time to get to second base. Angle your body so you face the teammate fielding the ball. This position will make it easier to catch the ball and throw it to first.

AVOID THE BASE RUNNER

The base runner will slide into second base hard to try to take your feet out. There are two ways to avoid the base runner. You can touch second base, then step to the left of the base to throw to first. Or you can step on second base, then jump over the runner while throwing the ball.

If the ball is hit to the left side of the infield, the second baseman must turn the double play. This is a very difficult play. To turn two as a second baseman, put your left foot on the back of the base. Then push off from the base when you throw. This move will protect you from the charging runner.

77 HOW TO HOLD A RUNNER ON BASE

A good baserunner is always trying to get a big lead off base without getting caught. Follow these tips and the runner won't get too far. If you develop a good **pickoff** move, you might throw out a few runners.

DEVELOP A PICKOFF MOVE

A good pickoff move is a pitcher's ultimate weapon against base runners. A quick and accurate throw keeps runners close to the base. And if they get too far away, you can pick them off.

↳ **pickoff**—when the pitcher throws to a baseman and the runner

SLIDE STEP

The slide step is used to get the ball to the catcher quickly. To throw a slide step pitch, don't kick your leg up into the air as in a normal pitch. Just step toward the catcher and throw. It's much harder for a runner to steal when the ball gets to the plate quickly.

"The idea with the slide step … is that you find a comfortable way to maintain your pitching rhythm and keep your form. You don't want to simply rush the ball to the plate to help stop the running game."
–TIM HUDSON, PITCHER, ATLANTA BRAVES

New York Yankees pitcher Andy Pettitte has one of the best pickoff moves in major-league history. The Tampa Bay Rays' Carl Crawford is one of the best base stealers in the game. But even Crawford plays it safe when Pettitte is on the mound. "We pretty much shut it down when at first base when we go against Andy," Crawford said. "We can't tell if he's going home or to first base. He has such a good move."

The Pickoff Artist

There's a lot of ground to cover in the outfield. As an outfielder, you can't let the ball get behind you. And once you get the ball, you need to get it to the infield as quickly as possible. Here are a couple of tips for getting to the ball and getting it in.

TAKE A STEP BACK

When the ball is hit toward you, take a few steps back and see where the ball is going. Your main goal is to keep the ball in front of you. It's easier to come in on a fly ball than to go back. Backing up a few steps prepares you for a ball hit over your head.

KEEP YOUR GLOVE DOWN AND RUN

Once you see where the ball is going, run hard toward it with your arms pumping. For better speed, keep your glove tucked in. Don't reach out to catch the ball until you know you can grab it.

HIT THE CUTOFF

After fielding the ball, throw the ball accurately to the **cutoff**. Hitting the cutoff can be hard if you caught the ball running away from the infielder. If this happens, stop and plant your feet. This will help you throw the ball on target.

All pro baseball players made it to the big leagues through practice, patience, and hard work. Don't get discouraged if you make a mistake. Even pros like Hanley Ramirez and Tim Lincecum make mistakes. Keep working on the tips and advice you've learned in this book. Maybe one day you can play just like the pros!

"The only people not making errors are the ones not on the field."
-OZZIE GUILLEN, MANAGER, CHICAGO WHITE SOX

↳ cutoff—an infielder who takes the throw in from an outfielder

GLOSSARY

CHANGEUP—a pitch that looks like a fastball, but is much slower, causing the batter to swing too early

CURVEBALL—a pitch with a lot of spin that changes direction while in the air, often causing the batter to miss

CUTOFF—an infielder who takes the throw in from an outfielder

DELIVERY—the arm and leg motions a pitcher uses while winding up and making a pitch

DOUBLE PLAY—when the fielding team gets two outs in one play

FASTBALL—a straight, fast pitch that often travels faster than 90 miles per hour

PICKOFF—when the pitcher throws to a base and the runner is tagged out before returning to the base

SACRIFICE BUNT—a bunt used to move runners to the next base

STANCE—the position of a player's feet and body

READ MORE

Cook, Sally, and James Charlton. *Hey Batta Batta Swing!: The Wild Old Days of Baseball.* New York: M.K. McElderry Books, 2007.

Dreier, David Louis. *Baseball: How it Works.* The Science of Sports. Mankato, Minn.: Capstone Press, 2010.

McMahon, Dave. *Baseball Skills: How to Play Like a Pro.* How to Play Like a Pro. Berkeley Heights, N.J.: Enslow Publishers, 2009.

INTERNET SITES

FactHound offers a safe, fun way to find Internet sites related to this book. All of the sites on FactHound have been researched by our staff.

Here's all you do:

Visit *www.facthound.com*

Type in this code: 9781429648240

INDEX ⌐